UPEND

CLAIRE MEUSCHKE

UPEND

UPEND
UPEND
UPEND
UPEND
UPEND
UPEND
UPEND
UPEND
UPEND
UPEND

NOEMI PRESS

Published by Noemi Press

www.noemipress.org

Copyright © 2020 by Claire Meuschke

All rights reserved

Noemi Press titles are distributed to the trade by

Small Press Distribution

Phone (510) 524-1668

ISBN 978-1-934819-87-6

Cover design by Jeffrey Pethybridge

Cover art by Linda Infante Lyons. *Anipa* © 2019

Interior design by Diana Arterian

Printed in the United States of America

9 8 7 6 5 4 3 2 1

First edition

Noemi Press

To my great-grandmother, who the archive elides

LIST OF ILLUSTRATIONS

UPEND

FIND AND EXPLORE

Likeable Sand 6058	Angels Camp	Chinese Red 0057
Olde World Gold 7700	Chino	Indian White 0035
Edgy Gold 6409	Eureka	Vintage Gold 9024
Agreeable Gray 7029	Fortuna	Restrained Gold 6129
Ancestral Gold 6407	Imperial	Hunt Club 6468
Moderate White 6140	Indian Wells	Indigo 6531
Escapade Gold 6132	Indio	Well-Bred Brown 7027
Cotton White 7104	Industry	Independent Gold 6401
Mossy Gold 6139	Redlands	Relic Bronze 6403
Divine White 6105	Los Angeles	Golden Rule 6383
Neutral Ground 7568	Mariposa	Adaptive Shade 7053
Original White 7077	Orange	Humble Gold 6380
Quilt Gold 6696	Oroville	Different Gold 6396
Hong Mon See Shee	Birth name	translated to Chinese to English

SW 6401
Independent Gold

View Details

SW 6383
Golden Rule

View Details

SW 2814
Rookwood Antique Gold

View Details

SW 6388
Golden Fleece

View Details

SW 7700
Olde World Gold

View Details

SW 7679
Golden Gate

View Details

SW 6677
Goldenrod

View Details

SW 9019
Golden Plumeria

View Details

SW 6905
Goldfinch

View Details

SW 2824
Renwick Golden Oak

View Details

SW 6664
Marigold

View Details

Name of Father Hong Wing
Name of Mother (before Marriage)
Unknown (Indian)

NEUTRAL GROUND 7568

Unknown <Indian> covers my great-grandmother
on my grandfather's birth certificate
she was from Alaska and died in San Francisco, CA
after her Chinese husband was stabbed

the paint company Sherwin-Williams has over forty names
to describe any shade—brown to yellow to grey—as gold
their logo reads "cover the earth"
see paint blood drip
down earth head
land pulled off at the crown

my great-grandfather's headline in *The San Francisco Call*—
CHINAMAN DECOYED TO ROOM AND SLAIN

No. 135, HONG ON   Inspr..... C. E.Ebey
Native (Visaed)   Inter..... Chin Jack
Ex S.S.Korea, 7-15-12   Steno..... F.E.Field

STATEMENT OF APPLICANT - - - - - - - - - - - - - - - SWORN

Applicant speaks Sam Yup dialect - Interpreter speaks See
Yip dialect originally, qualified in Sam Yup

-- oOo --

Q What is your name? A. Hong On; Hong On Ling; no other name; not married
Q How old are you? A. 17
Q When were you born? A.K. S.21-2-2, in San Francisco, 23 Ross Alley
Q Who told you that? A. My grandmother told me
Q Have you any documentary evidence to produce in support of that statement?
A. I don't know; I have not anything
Q What is your father's name? A. Hong Bock Wing; I don't know his marriage
name
Q Did you ever hear him called by any other name at all? A. No
Q Do you know what his milk name was? A. This is his milk name
Q Where is your father now? A. He died
Q When and how? A.K. S. 25 - Sullivan Alley
Q What caused his death? A. I don't know, but he had been sick I don't
know how long
Q Didn't you ever hear what caused your father's death? A.No
Q What is your mother's name? A. She is an Indian
Q Where is she? A. She died
Q When and where? A. K. S. 25 also in San Francisco, I don't know the address
Q How long have you lived in San Francisco? A. I departed for China K. S. 28,
I was born in K. S. 21; I have stayed in China until now
Q What were you doing while you were living in San Francisco? A. Nothing, never
went to school in San Francisco
Q With whom did you live while you were in San Francisco? A. Brother of my
grandmother, Ng Wing, also known as Ng Sik Heung
Q Where did you live with him? A. 6th street, Oakland, I don't remember the
number
Q Do you know how long you lived with him? A.I don't remember how long - ever
since my parents died
Q Who took you to China? A. My uncle, Ng Wing
Q Have you lived with him all the while since you were in China? No, I
was living with my paternal grandmother, Ng Wing returned to the U. S.
Q What is your paternal grandmother's name? A. Ng Shee
Q Have you any brothers or sisters? A. No brothers, two sisters, one died
and one is married
Q What was the name of the sister that died? A. Hong Jung Ho
Q Didn't you ever hear that you had had a brother? A. I never heard about it
Q Your sister, Jung Oy, says that you had a brother who was given away by
your mother in his infancy? A. I never heard about it

17

Q Do you remember at what address you lived with Ng Wing in San Francisco?
  A. No, I don't know

Q Then how do you know you lived with him? A. He took me to China. I went
  to him after my parents died

Q Don't you remember anything about theplace where he lived? A. To my
  best recollection it was on the 3d floor over So Chung & Co., Dupont
  Street

Q Do you remember any of the other streets of Chinatown, San Francisco?
  A. I could not remember such a long time

Q Do you remember any important events that happendd when you were living in
  San Francisco? A. Nothing

Q Do you know where your sister Jung Ho died? A. No

Q What was your father's business? A. I don't know, he died when I was only
  5 years old

Q In what village did you live while you were in China? A. Moy Chun village,
  Mow Gong, Nam Hoy district

Q Did your sister write to you any while you were in China? A. No

Q Did you write to her any? A. Yes, I wrote to her before I came

Q What have you been doing in China? A.Student

Note (Identifies all photographs)

Q Have you anything further to state? A. No

Q Have you understood the interpreter? A. Yes

Note (Interpreter Park asked the applicant if he had understood the inter-
  preter in the case and the answer was in the affirmative)

8-6-12
Signed:

-- oOo --

         caught myself wading in the past
a sound layer of at least three different birds
Wednesday bins roll to curb   old smashed glass
the dog sulks
      dangles head and front paws off the bed
didn't take her low growl seriously
guideless together
           make scratch on paper
            store sounds we yawn

        I can spend the whole day
        shaking whiteflies off
month-old squash leaves
I leave   unalike nature

          dream ahead of silvery blue
          squash plump
April's last new moon   I try to film the circumference of
     Angel Island
        wild horses? with my lens a buckskin
             ran down
      a cliff to a black one
     felt from ocean west
          at eastward angle
musk oxen protect their young at the center
I don't have any words for the past question

WOUND STUDY

so often we point to a bright planet
before stars after
       the sun's gone and wonder
           half-hearted
           which one it is

October   don't know where you came from or
where I'll be when you come again

unfamiliar with memorized month names
can't place to real time
like anatomy lines connect words to gun parts
like unfamiliar Latin plant words *slanted*
       taken internally? meant for silence on placard
       a privilege to be timeless

CLEARING

I don't believe in luck though I find myself saying
that's lucky as a filler for silence   or merely
                              that's that

twice now the coffee cup bottom has filtered
a semi-evergreen forest in all its ground sludge
to say get out of the desert or don't

read about the flammability of buffalo poop
read a sign about the massacre of buffalo during
Indian Removal Act not the massacre of Indians
                         during buffalo removal

comet moths feed on poison ivy whereas
morpho butterflies leave banners of blue
afterimages on dark foliage

when I take off my clothes I think now
might be the time to start anti-gravity poses

once mastering hand stands I can
repopulate my cells   then precede myself

FIGURATIVE AS LITERAL

someone can replace someone with a like or as
someone can replace someone without a like or as
replacement can mean literally relocated
or figuratively placed in a hole

like side-by-side without the like
is still side-by-side

birds made homes out of trees and then we did

associated or dissociated
a figure is real
a number is literate
products like people
come with a number and a name

I would hope that reading this in reverse would
image like a mirror
like history as a way to remember doesn't image

LESSEN

I learned English on top of an estimated
fifty buried languages
I can dig just inches down and find
obsidian and shells
original daily life
a plum tree produced
overseas thus underdeveloped plums

through language I learned
to disembody my own body
my head hurts as if severed
I learned to relate surroundings to the self
my older sister my twin brother
my best friend my plum tree
my sister ran away
his hands around her neck
see this without eyes
I can possess
I can make a claim
sister brother friend tree
let's let what surrounds surround

QUICK VIEW

colors hint on agricultural drip lines along the highway
see through butterfly guts on the windshield

alongside the snowmelt pond
the dog sweeps herself a hole
I feed her one blackberry
she spits and rolls over high-like

skip stones not to get ahead
to see water make a point

one butterfly black mostly blue
when the sun hits

the dog Mica rolls
in mica shining
in her name

promise: you can discover long-lasting

QUICK VIEW

said it *must be nice to drink water while swimming*
like that
said statements
like *it's a beautiful day*
said *sadly barely staying afloat*

the colonist in a clearing
said something
is like something
bodies like dirt
become dirt

titles like heads are lines like bodies
waiting a turn

review: are you discontinuing that shade? we're sorry

this is where your wildest dreams dream billboard is like the pause for

gold like the assumption there's more than like the edge of the Pacific

like eucalyptus lines El Camino like roots warp pavement white painted

child bike like Mission Bell symbol like we crossed to explorers Balboa

Ave to Cortez to Cabrillo to Drake to Bernal to Vancouver to De Soto

to Columbus like avenue means to go toward to arrive like a blacktop

covered in nineties tricolor neon of the United States map where like

same color won't touch to isolate states distinct like tag where

California was a base so long like to touch in a game is to kill I feared

Alaska so far and big like flour babies like kids threw rocks at the girl's

head covered like like the technological rush like like hands pan full of

silicon dust for new applications to push whose lineage out like like the

19th century over and over

THE SCENT OF HERBS IS A PLANT SCREAMING IN FLAMES

just when you remark to yourself how temperate
                                    water feels
a little white snake wraps around your calf
                        a pattern of stable vortices
cinches its jaw to its own body
            the snake is heavier than its visual mass
you try to swim up to the river's surface
but your head sinks with the image of fangs

the snake could be a metaphor for the patriarchy
easy now   a simmer
                        or an oil pipeline leaking venom
                            into the Missouri River
but for now the snake is a snake

no one tells you how lonely drowning is

the secret to painting a convincing glare

add rosemary flowers at the end
collect droplets on the lid for neck and face
when you realize all your metaphors are literal
when you could be you or you or me
                        wasn't that you
when all the children cried
put your face up to the dead rattlesnake

cut off the rattler you kept
in a Ziploc later moved to the closet to the trash when
                            embarrassed

a boiling pot is water's maximum freedom

SW 6396 Different Gold	SW 6403 Escapade Gold	SW 0009 Eastlake Gold	SW 6670 Gold Crest	SW 6380 Humble Gold	SW 6382 Ceremonial Gold
View Details	View Details	View Details	View Details	View Details	View Details
SW 6409 Edgy Gold	SW 6367 Viva Gold	SW 6139 Mossy Gold	SW 6368 Bakelite Gold	SW 6370 Saucy Gold	SW 6698 Kingdom Gold
View Details	View Details	View Details	View Details	View Details	View Details

-- oOo --

A protection spell? Imprisonment? Orientation?

The symbol above appears on page 27 of my grandfather Hong On's immigration trial at Angel Island where he was detained in 1912. In 2012, my twin and I uncovered the trial, specimens through glass, holding those stunted pencils reserved for federal and state buildings—reading our grandfather's testimony as if with him. We were only miles away from his mother's grave, which we got lost trying to find. She was the only Native body in the Chinese cemetery. The United States is a relatively recent name with nervously sketched borders. We belong to this official territory wholly, precariously.

Hong On was 17 years old when he returned from China to California. He was orphaned by age five at the turn of the century in San Francisco when his Chinese father was stabbed and his Alaska Native mother from an unnamed tribe died of unknown causes in the Gum Moon mission home for women and children. He was sent to live with relatives in rural, southern China. One sister died in infancy, while his other sister was disabled and was raised in Gum Moon. During Hong On's trial on Angel Island, the transcribed Q-and-A informs my grandfather of his loss; that he had an infant brother who was given away—statements with question marks: *Didn't you know? Didn't anybody ever tell you?* These revelations hemorrhaged out a vague family story.

The above symbol heads one of the transcribed court trials as a numberless number or a transcriber's doodle. Throughout the archive, there are peculiar and seemingly rushed marks like the misspelled, typewritten word *deth* alongside of the alleged mother with four x's obscuring each letter and the corrected *death* spelling typed above. *deth* *death*.

The -- oOo -- symbol conjures less loss and less error. Each shape remains intact. The centered zero or letter O gets two servants or children or gems—or they're equal in scale to the central figure, but just off in the distance, there and not here, better off, not dead center. The double hyphens are wings? Borders? There are no angels—only heavy islands attached to heavy islands called states, called reservations, called national parks.

I use the em dash when I can't bear for the sentence to end.
Here they punctuate the symbol into existence.

Give first arrival and all subsequent trips:

First arrival _____ *Only trip*

Departed _____

Returned _____

Departed _____

Returned _____

Departed _____

Returned _____

Did you register? (if not, give reasons) *No.*

Have you any other papers showing your right to be and remain in
the United States? *No.*

ALTAR

moths may orient celestially or
        are thrown off by our light
I catch five and don't dislike the feel
        of feet on my palms

I throw them into the dark so I
don't see what happens happen

moth balls he said
tentative around my feelings
when I said the smell was like
all my aunts' homes

naphthalene caught between
earth and one star in Perseus

this is not a star atlas
I wander too much to
wonder and alter

the healer guest speaker
burns cedar
says it starts when it starts

COUNTER

renovate the kitchen landscape maple whose leaves turned
purple and fell many times a year transplanted from Japan

we sat in after eating sour grass the government can afford
to send seeds to the moon to plant in national forests

give moon trees names and plaques over whose
dead body I'll stare into this estate sale abalone shell

she'll email but I think of snails I'll wait for a technology
crash and I'll wait a burned-out offering until I feel better

bitterness the pastor who drives the Uber for supplemental cash
is what he wrote his book on while I read about penicillin

leeched from tan oak but what happens concurrently is silent
he won't elaborate on bitterness and I don't ask

how an island detainee's scanned photocopied trial
becomes held and how as this cutting do I plant it

ALTAR

a place that imports its marble as mass kitchen and grave alike
is no place for me yet here I am handing myself a sponge

COUNTER

is this portable form
medicine to take
well take
it it's yours

held thing
becomes a thing in

the wrong hands
potent
I dispossess

words stated:
California
Angel
Status
Alleged

ALTAR

maybe there's no place to memorize grief
script slants to signal what is my opaque
oranges illuminated cubbied
under whole catfish we'll eat
for the New Year we're
half a year late to celebrate

a date is no place
where my hands never held
your dirt
where do headstones come from?
give me
a mountain to look down history

how high a surface makes an altar?
a book face-up
spine-out
what can I place on it to make it
work?

CHINAMAN DECOYED TO ROOM AND SLAIN

Hong Ah Wing Is Stabbed to Death and Chen Hoot Kee Is Accused.

MAN WHO WAS STABBED TO DEATH AND THE ONE WHO IS SUS-
PECTED OF HAVING BEEN INSTRUMENTAL IN HIS DEATH; ALSO
PLACE WHERE THE STABBING OCCURRED.

e died (murdered)

STUNNING ANGEL ISLAND FIRE SEEN FOR MILES

The military planted 24 acres of eucalyptus that expanded to 86 and
invaded native plants.

Chinese characters carved into a prison wall in the Immigration Station:
Once you see the open net, why throw yourself in? It is only
because of empty pockets I can do nothing else.
— UNKNOWN

Before historical; before conservationists; before the military;
before quarantine; before the Immigration Station—what systems did
the Miwok use for their livelihood? Livelihood; not survival.

In 1915 the military introduced mule deer for recreational
hunting.

Surviving is everything after.

Eucalyptus trees are highly flammable. Flaming debris from the island
caused the Oakland fire in 1991 when I was a one-year-old. My family
told stories about where they were that day like the 1989 earthquake.
My mother; pregnant with my brother and me; rolling a cart; canned
food falling.

A semicolon is clipped as a means to continue.

The 1906 earthquake caused fires for days. Immigration files
were destroyed.

In 2008 residents described the flames as red as orange as yellow.
Conclusion: the island was a fort and later an immigration station; is
now reachable; a popular picnicking and camping spot.

In 2012 I danced in the bar with the old man who sang on the G train
platform—dry mouth on mouth kiss I gave him the
eucalyptus pod from my coat pocket held for when I missed
California as invasive as it was.

In 1993 California State Parks discovered a market in Japan for
eucalyptus mulch, which reduced the cost of eucalyptus removal.

Prisoners from San Quentin labored over the burned slash piles.

Garlon 4 Herbicide was applied to cut stumps.

A federal plaque is the afterimage of a headstone.

In 1775 Juan de Ayala named the island. He and his naval crew were the first Europeans to access it.

In third grade we learned about Christopher Columbus, and while the teacher talked, I could see the sliced Achilles heels infected— copper tokens around the necks for those who found gold.

A ferry ticket costs 15 dollars roundtrip.

Put coins in the cemented-down binoculars. See everything except the place itself.

Introductory

turies of stifling gregariousness. They like crowds and clamor and elbow-jostling. Ten bunks in a room twelve by eight was their idea of social contact. . . . With a Chinese population today over fifty per cent American born, two blocks of China-town still remain the most densely populated in the whole of San Francisco.

Perhaps it is a familiarity with dense living that makes the Chinese such masters of arrangement. Give any Chinaman a half-dozen oranges, a couple of newly laid eggs and a green pepper and they will fall instinctively into a picture as he lays them on the kitchen table. If he empties a tub of salt fish and puts it out on the back landing, and throws a ravished rice sack of matting and two discarded ginger jars beside it, you will have a perfect study in still life. He has had to conserve space, he has had to conserve funds, he has had to conserve time. Ordinary people in such situations conserve, or more properly they stifle, beauty. But the Chinese are not ordinary people. They love beauty and if they cannot in-dulge their taste for art with Ming vases, they create art sub-consciously out of ordinary materials of life—food, frag-ments, even refuse.

Once before the earthquake and fire, I boarded at a bache-lor club. We had a very good Chinese cook and one night we decided to give a dinner party—to invite some of our women friends to taste his quality. At the last moment, some-body discovered that since it had been nobody's business to attend to flowers for the table, none were in evidence. We scolded Hong about it, although he was in nowise to blame. He merely grunted.

But when we came into the dining-room after cocktails, there were flowers—bouquets of ravishing beauty at either end of the table. On a sunless back terrace were a couple of stunted fuchsia bushes, a red geranium or two, a volun-teer cineraria. Out of a clash of red and pink and violent purple, Hong had evolved two formal masses of flowers springing conically out of as many mason fruit jars. They were not only triumphs of art—they were triumphs of art evolved from scraps of blossoms. They rivaled the dinner. Soon after, Hong was shot down in Chinatown by a rival gunman. It was alleged that he was a highbinder, himself. . . . How many white gangsters could be trusted to take a handful of fuchsia blossoms, mix them with some geranium petals and a cluster of cineraria bloom and evolve things of beauty for a formal dinner party?

It was not so much that the interpreters of San Francisco's Chinatown drew false pictures but that they drew pictures without real substance. They concocted posters, really, in flat tones, as if their real desire was to "sell" Chinatown. All the vengeance and clamor and color of the Orient were in the Chinese quarter unmistakably. But so were simplicity, and calm, and sanity. The authors gave us hatchetmen with fingers on the triggers of guns, never hatchetmen weaving flowers into table decorations. They must have had such incidents, but they either voted them incongruous or ineffective.

When the idea came to me to gather together fragments of Chinese incident into a more or less coherent account, in my zeal to be just to my yellow neighbor, I made a fleeting resolution to soft pedal violence and lust and cruelty. These points, concerning the Chinese, had been stressed too emphatically by my predecessors. But I had not progressed far before I realized that such notes had been struck not too loudly but too unintelligently. What was needed was not less emphasis but more understanding. One would miss half the point of gangster violence in America in the lush twenties, unless one had some appreciation of the events which brought gangsters into power during that period. So with the delinquencies of Chinatown. Highbinder wars, slave-girls,

-- oOo --

metaphora
>   to carry across
>   to transfer
>   especially from one word to another word

what the grief is like

there's implicit movement
like imperialism and like survival

humility is a literal metaphor
being at the level of humus earth
I use it up from state to state

Senecas found oil
cupped it from the surface of earth
to bind wounds
the United States is one big bust town
Angel Island is a wound covered in plaque

dream wherein
        I'm encased in a clear tub
under a guest bed in my home?
                doorbell rings door opens
    strain to remember if I'm victim or trespasser

    fell asleep with emeralds in my ears again
I was pre-Columbian
        a male big shot warrior
        a village requested for help

      see me and two others
all on horseback racing up a mountain

    I puked up yellow liquid after asking
        the caretaker to put green sprouts on my
        forehead   stems in bouquet form
        unlike a crown

-- oOo --

two figures travel by foot during the 19th century
bird's-eye-view of tiny settlements along a river

I become the woman
my husband has his arm around my waist
sweeping me almost across the ground
we're white and fleeing from some mistake

he begins painting my nails bright red
I'm annoyed at how they look
clumped and on my finger-skin
I fear someone will notice I'm not her

this is me living or not living
the idiom
blood on our hands

19th century colonial women
suffered nationally a leg paralysis
Western science called it psychosis
            what about immobilizing guilt
                    organized resistance
                    the land not wanting you?

-- oOo --

dull the edges while try to be visible
          men growing up left
nail clippings anywhere
          never knew when
you'd get pierced

track history without
the hunt man
          undo bullet points or
          deadlines
observe a live thing live
          tell a side mirror

over the Ancestral Gold 6407 Bay Bridge a
          story through my mom and dad and
          their moms and dads

think at the water the island
          before knowing one was
ever held there
          think your own mouth tell
a memorized story

not held but detained
          captive
          seized
not one but many

the water it's clear
can't see through it

me in a peopled place
looking like a question to ask

we hit a bird or a bird flies
into the windshield

-- oOo --

stranger at the conference said her stranger-
father would have called me a Heinz 57 variety
                    after the facilitator smudges us
            an ice break favorite movie
suicide statistics
                    we all get up and do
                            the Electric Slide
            wayward limbs
            think I'm more
            Dum Dums Mystery
                    splintered in mouth watering
                    factory-seamed

MILK NAME

apple pineapple pine apple
pineapple pine apple pine
apple pineapple pine apple
pineapple pine apple pine
apple pineapple pine apple
pineapple pine apple pine

-- oOo --

two bored and diligent angels crown a virgin
rolling her eyes

what's happening in your DNA
            happened seven generations ago
and will happen seven generations after

in a bowl of water I watch
a dried mushroom enliven

circle around the head to bring out the
            head-like qualities of the head
shared air between here and the outer air
like Buddha with an orb behind the head
            in repose
            personal paradise
I don't put anything on my head
planets don't follow me around when you look
happy to have a head

words are empty space
stars cut sight
words are the central figure
surrounded by space
stars cut sight

words represent themselves as well as
the cut around the circumference of their heads

in 1850 California
the state funded bullets for volunteer killers
the price for an Indian scalp
was at least 10 dollars

-- oOo --

an altar is an altar
if there's a rectangle next to it with words
an altar is an altar
if you talk silently towards it

framed Harvest Gold 2858
wood-carved foliage
brushed with bundled animal hair
molten earth

wall the self and words
matter me

-- oOo --

hang on the wall
sight the eight-point star

    gold on the teal shroud of an Italian gothic virgin
                        compass rose
    quilts mass-produced and hand-made
    not on the police badge worn as tin heart

      failure to locate the grave of the alleged mother

      Lakota Morning Star
    Star of Bethlehem held by an angel
        Texas Lone Star
     Mayan cross of Quetzalcoatl

      failure to locate the grave of the alleged mother

   Eight Immortals of China
     Seal of Solomon
     Star of Lakshmi
Wiccan Wheel of the Year

      failure to locate the grave of the alleged mother

four corners of space
    bloodroot
  lesser celandine
Goldenrod 6677

CENSUS

Restrained Gold 6129

Mossy Gold 6139

Harvest Gold 2858

Ancestral Gold 6407

Monarch Gold 2920

Olde World Gold 7700

Goldenrod 6677

Marigold 6664

Golden Gate 7679

Golden Plumeria 9019

Quilt Gold 6696

Folksy Gold 6360

Edgy Gold 6409

Vintage Gold 9024

Escapade Gold 6132

Independent Gold 6401

Humble Gold 6380

Different Gold 6396

Relic Bronze 6403

Chivalry Copper 6353

Artifact 6138

Reliable White 6091

Original White 7077

Intimate White 6322

Moderate White 6140

Welcome White 6658

Nice White 6063

Reserved White 7056

Everyday White 6077

High Reflective White 7757

Paperwhite 7105

Modest White 6084

Divine White 6105

Free Spirit 6973

Polite White 6056

Spatial White 6259

Indian White 0035
Chinese Red 0057
Red Cent 6341
Reddened Earth 6053
Agreeable Gray 7029
Suitable Brown 7054
Well-Bred Brown 7027
Rugged Brown 6062
Nearly Brown 9093
Less Brown 6040
Resort Tan 7550
Colonial Revival Tan 2828
Colonial Yellow 0030
New Colonial Yellow 2853
Chopsticks 7575
Diverse Beige 6079
Neutral Ground 7568
Adaptive Shade 7053

Q A.

Q   ? A.   ?

Q   ? A.

Q
Q A.

Q   ? A.

Q Q   ? A.

Q Q   ? A.   ?

Q   ? A.

Q Q Q   ? A.

Q Q   ? A.   ? A.

Q Q   ? A.

Q   ? A.

I don't know; I have not anything
                              name   I don't know
name
                                    any other name at all?   No
                        name   name
                              died

          death?   I don't know   I don't
know
                                              death?   No
              name?
              died

                                              I don't know

                                                            Nothing

              also known as
                                            I don't remember the
number
                                    I don't remember how long - ever
          died

                                                          No, I

                        name?
                        No   died

          name   died?
Didn't you ever   I never heard

              I never heard

```
        remember
    No, I don't know
Then how do you know
                        died

Don't you remember anything
best recollection

Do you remember any
    I could not remember such a long time
Do you remember any
                    Nothing
    know                            died     No
                                I don't know      died


                                                        No



                        No


            the answer was in the affirmative


Signed:
```

mistletoe grows in measures
kilometers from the border
clumped on cottonwoods along
a dried river near a little compound
no one in sight and me not
wanting enough out of serenity
if a fire takes the prairie it's fine
pictures shown of roots

surpassing symmetry into soil
a compass weed waves down
we trip over our own shoes
somewhere a lover tugs a collar
wanting the heart to fit tighter
has to be done and not allowed on
paper like weather happening
did I wake you? every time
I answer the phone and meant

sky to stay this light longer
make a day of it no sunken urgency
where forecasters speak
conditionally and are always right
not where I dream of Alaska seen
through the glass of a lucent gondola
the hand had to touch to make sure
was there when skimming palm tree
tops and glacier ponds the dreamer
woke because I didn't believe

```
  ?
   ?
  Q
 ?Q
  Q

  ?

  Q
  Q
 Q
 Q
 Q
 Q
 Q

  Q   Didn't you ever hear what caused your father's death?  A.No
  Q   What is your mother's name?  A. She is an Indian
  Q   Where is she?  A. She died
  Q
  Q

  Q

  Q

  Q

  Q

  Q
  Q

  ?
  Q
```

```
  Q   a young buck crosses the trail old
  Q   enough to be alone and continue into the
  Q   same plane cholla prickly pear saguaro
 QQ   flowers I don't know the names for
 QQ   yellow and purple beneath ranges of snow
 QQ   beneath a grocery list I wrote I always
  Q   ask what I don't mean he says
  Q   your dog looks like a nice dog
  Q   not too scary but scary enough
  Q   I have to agree as I descend
  Q   out of sight still form a question
 QQ   for the stranger stemmed up the tripod
 QQ   like what do you take pictures of
  Q   is it the view?
```

Oct. 15, 1912.

Chinese Inspector in Charge,

    Immigration Service,

        Angel Island.

Sir:

    In re Hong On, Native, San Francisco, No. 135 Ex SS
      "Korea", July 12, 1912, landed on parole:

    The record room in its report of October 10th verifies
the death of the alleged father. Verification of the death
of the alleged mother can not be made on account of the inability
of the witnesses to give sufficient data for an intelligent
search.

    Attorney Straus in his letter of September 5th, 1912,
states that he will furnish a man who can point out the grave
of the alleged mother if necessary.

        Respectfully,

                Chinese Inspector.

THM

CHINA MARY

1

magenta glow of deforested timber
red stitches on the inlet
women math with hands to be marked unknown
glass display box well-dusted
silver mixture is an eye trick
two opposites on the wheel cancel
out into muddy gray
gentle how the crow lands next to another crow
eucalyptus branch to palm frond   invasive
invasive out the corner of an eye you
clear cut the upturned creosote roots
a good place to birth
quiet snake among dry sage leaves rattling
their absent water
they named anyone China Mary
so she was China Mary

2

so late she's early to the cultural reawakening
rose from the Pacific a beached whale vertebrae
some celestial body   *celestial* is a privileged
word for *outside*
propped on a dashboard   nonetheless
is three dumb words that cancel
China Mary doesn't wear a halo
she adorns herself in watermark
dust mote her own hairline
shapely around her skull
how unorthodox what the devout did
photos that don't exist make a mirror of rock
China Mary doesn't like how she got here
but she's here nonetheless in
Sitka Portland San Francisco Tombstone
with brown eyes
green or red depending on you
black eyes in photos she wants
to look at something up close for a lifetime

3

mail-ordered escapee she sleeps on
a mattress of spruce boughs encaved in canyon wall
makes jook by the cauldron cast iron
her peasant skin an unbelievable flat affect
how they feared her gold projection
the men cut her heels so she couldn't run away
showed her her worth
was to stop creation of her whole kind
the wet opacity of seal eyes
ambiguous lip curl
black hair turned technicolor in sun
how many squirrels make up her garment
countless she
so large or small we can't see her
I want you to close your eyes and imagine
that that's the story
you won't tell the children you'll never have
they tried to see through her the way
she used animal oil inflamed to see through dark

4

nonetheless a family throws factory potato chips
into the sea for a full-blown loss whale tour
one color on a screen is comprised of three
magenta is as natural as a purple rose bouquet
on a plastic grocery bag is as natural as China Mary
how to search and research the dark past
in brightly lit scatter
China Mary left me nothing
which is why she's still here
ignoring me at the checkout counter in my dream
sidestepping my conversation about Alaska
she isn't my great-grandmother or my mother or me
strangers that year would tell me I looked like someone else

5

they wheeled out the monitors in rainbows like candy
for our dirt-lined child hands
we learn names for shapes colors numbers
the man who walks to and from the bus perpetually
holding up his pants
the man who bends and stares wide-eyed into the traffic
the emaciated Abraham Lincoln look-alike
dust swirls around pigeon-toed siblings in pairs
a flood to say about their dog who farts
their fathers who will return

6

when the world broke the world didn't say
it's not you it's me
and that's how I knew it was me ending
you woke me in your sleep to say
every day every day every day
I wanted to smell like a pine forest
but I smell like gerbil bedding
fixate on CD-ROM reflections on the wall
outside see China Mary transcending
the transcendentalists   a photoshoot
a massacre of images and their copies
a prolonged hand shake with the president
her opacity is blinding the men with her non-halo
fast food cups protect cacti from frost and will
stay in the earth longer than us
I want us to stay like that awhile
watch the compost slide off her bones so gently
she's not rising or sinking and that's why they're afraid

GET WELL SOON

the room is brass and amber and green
men statuesque look like there's live music

there's no live music   commodity I'm unworthy
boys throw pennies at me   the fountain

hold your breath until you're out of the tunnel
that is a double rainbow you want with your eyes to be under

I smell normal candles on any day and think of the birthday
we didn't have that year of the snake-horse in Albuquerque
everyone seemed to wish everyone would get home safe

I was on crutches and a guy with his beer-glazed mouth
took my fingers to his jeans to push them against
the metal bolt in his shin to say it could be worse

REDDISH BLUISH

one word against another
one word word against against another
one word word word against against against another
as we speak in peripherals we order the chaos
trees communicate disease through their root system
against another you can feel the accumulation inevitably
say I believe in the beauty of crystals
say beauty can heal and crystals aren't magical for that

my sister's biological sister somewhere is named Crystal
mine a meaning for clear
so that from my sister's vantage I'm one outcome
comparable the way a life unfolds one way or else another
how film records the sculptor removing
three centimeters from the face
to save the image of the girl child against
a window hung crystal's multicolored
light fractals appear flat

shades that skip along the spectrum become a single red
the red is against what we know to be true

POSSESSION

bones golden on the stove to be loved from solid to liquid
imagined little yellow house   steamy pots   blue tiles
frantic birds dance fight on a branch to continue

dog pines her claw lines inside the front door for a return
I wear my teeth in my mouth for you   my heart on my heart
the ivy stem attaches to the blinds so they go up together

weed bouquets wind-bent are destined for outdoor tubs
whatever unintended sprout prolific beside the food source
I want the transmission to mend itself in time

mirrors on mirrors on foliage to multiply the day
to sit very still and not go bad

the perfect room: green-blue predominately
magenta flashes and a little three-dimensional cheer
violent how the birds hatch and seeds break the dirt

SW 6699
Crispy Gold

View Details

SW 6376
Gold Coast

View Details

SW 2831
Classical Gold

View Details

SW 6690
Gambol Gold

View Details

SW 6691
Glitzy Gold

View Details

SW 6696
Quilt Gold

View Details

SW 6398
Sconce Gold

View Details

SW 2858
Harvest Gold

View Details

SW 6904
Gusto Gold

View Details

SW 6360
Folksy Gold

View Details

SW 0012
Empire Gold

View Details

SW 7677
Gold Vessel

View Details

RESOLVE

They are, generally, better formed, and much more fleet,
than our common horses.

the past is specifically better-suited and much
more adorned than our everyday altar

the altar is a green glitch in a photo
or a magenta haze in a green terrain

I forgot it until I was told
the past is the change in shape you make

the narratives will not coalesce
or complement one another

any more than an afterimage must
exist on a white page

I WILL FURNISH A MAN

Among them, you will see every variety of color, imaginable,
from a jet black, to a snow white.

surrounding it you will see every variety of sight seeable
from a frozen hand to a vertebraed amber

      the past surrounds the altar
      you will see sight
      sight is from hand to amber
      a nation of tired receptors

if you wanted something shiny
go ahead
cry into
your own eye

US FLAG INVERTED

All the variety of colors found among our horses are
found among them, besides many varieties which are
never found among ours.

some of the variety of sights hidden surrounding our past
are hidden surrounding it beside many varieties which are
never hidden surrounding ours

      the sights surround our past
      the surrounding is hidden
      the sights are never hidden
      the sights are never ours

                                  yellow sky
                black stars
blood green

                blood brothers
held cutlery under a cold metal structure painted yellow

two humans leashing two cattle dogs
corralled by wild horses

WELCOME SIGN FACING IN

At this place also, as at the valley, there is a store,
at which large quantities of goods are daily sold,
by the missionaries, to both whites and Indians,
from which extensive profits are annually derived.

easier to break an object in two than in three
invisible store sold
heartbreak at which
seen today covered in glitter

put your pointer and thumb over
killer postcards at which
your baby's teeth jeweled

sold trinkets of your grandma's body
sold a tour guide to death sites
but the marks are one shade
the shape of California
a last cry death word
embedded in eyelids

KINDLY DISPOSITION WHEN BROKEN

The different farmers always keep a number of herdsmen,
whose business it is to drive the horses, from place to place,
as it becomes necessary, to seek additional pasturage,
and who are, usually, Indians or Mexicans of the lowest grade.

the numerous colonists always keep a variety of weapons
whose market it is to wipe the altars from place to place
as it becomes necessary to imagine place and who are usually
bound of the adjective noun

this is me making it
pathologically handed-
down dread

bouquet yourself a portrait in aggressive lilacs
a lifetime spent in the last stage of mourning

MOVED FOR CALIFORNIA WEATHER

The purity of the atmosphere is most extraordinary and almost incredible.
So pure is it in fact that flesh of any kind may be hung for weeks together
in the open air and that too in the summer season without undergoing putrefaction.

the texture of the trauma is most extraordinary and almost incredible
so textured is it in sensation that descendants of the continents may be
called for centuries together in the open air
and that too in timelessness without
out-bounding memorial
the texture is given a number
so textured without out-bounding
the texture is at blade point
so textured without memorial
the texture is a scalp
with a head and body

HYPNOTISM.

PROF. RAYMOND; teaches hypnotism & magnetic healing for $5; five lessons. 997 Market.

LOST AND FOUND.

LOST—Certificate No. 174 for 24 shares of capital stock of The National Ice Co., standing in the name of J. H. and M. Knief. Finder will please return same to The National Ice Co., 327 Market; reward.

LOST—A sunburst pin, diamond, surrounded by pearls, Fri. eve., Jan. 18, at Cotillion Hall or on Bush, bet. Octavia and Polk; liberal reward. Return 1707 Bush st.

LOST—A water spaniel dog Sunday at 122 Utah st., with white spot on breast and sore ear; liberal reward. Return to 122 Utah st.

LOST—Pair opera glasses, in fair leather case (Warner & Swasey make), between Sutter st. and Cliff House. Return to Cliff House and receive $5 reward.

LOST—A pair of gold lorgnettes on Jackson, Buchanan or Pacific ave. Return to 1817 Jackson st.; suitable reward.

LOST—Tuesday evening, one gold ring, light blue setting; liberal reward. Address 375 Fifth st.

LOST—Fawn and white greyhound. Return to 230 Laguna st. and receive reward.

LOST—Black beaded handbag, on Grant ave., near O'Farrell. Please leave at Call office.

LOST—Black cocker spaniel dog; tag No. 3637. Reward at 100 Minnesota st.

ANY old thing; also diamonds, sealskins; money on them; private entrance; perfect secrecy. UNCLE HARRIS, 15 Grant ave.

Wanted—Old gold for manufacturing. O. Nolte, jeweler, 348 O'Farrell, bet. Powell and Mason.

OLD gold, silver, diamonds and precious stones bought. J. R. JENKEL, 997 Market st.

STARE AT FOREST GREEN TO GET COCHINEAL ON THE PAGE

kids say mermaid hair   staying too long in a lake

algae-saturated   comparing strands to be most attractive   slimy
boy pronounced   mosquito with a *maw* sound in the gazebo

a new age woodsman with a pet bobcat approaches   says *that's tits*
                                 to every remark
                                 neutral to good

                      hard plastic cups smell burnt
                      between red and transparent

Yosemite printed on objects
                      in half-assed cursive

feeling bad for mules and donkeys who stay in the pen
                 while horses go out

disappointing tie-dye results   fireworks
I want my own Independence Day

Mariposa Battalion was federally hired to make   a human
clearing a pristine wonder   hunters green

they set fire to Ahwahnechee homes and heard the word *Yosemite*
thought the people were Yosemite   the word means killers

in Relic Bronze 6403   plaques   photos   voices over
I don't feel like talking   like I feel   I mean   voiced-over

TWO COLORS DIAMETRICALLY OPPOSED

what is recovery and what is recovered?

evoke the other on a white page

what is a safety?

didn't see a grandma ever so I didn't

see grandma's missing fingers

Agnes Hailstone's purple fingernails curl around a trigger

glint against the Arctic's grey-white

hallucinatory green

the candy factory took and took

a privilege we could choose any color for our rooms

say magenta is psychological

how the eyes compensate

I want a way

to be over recovery

though they were lightened to be less

brother's blue became a robin's egg

sister's terra cotta   a pumpkin

my teal   mint green

the ugly purple thong

my father gave me

an almost plastic sheen

St. Katherine of Karluk

how you hold the weight of orthodox

steel and make it look like

weightless moon through your eyes

"It is remarkable the erroneous idea the great majority of the outside world has of the tremendous extent of the valleys of the Yukon and its tributaries. While traveling up and down the river on the P. B. Weare I have frequently passed hundreds of nameless streams flowing into the river. They are not down upon any chart, have never had a place upon a map, and their size and extent neither the captain nor even the natives knew anything about, and upon the gravel of their shores a pick had never been struck. Hundreds of

FAR OUT MAN

with someone else's small talk about
                    another day's sunset
        pictures of sunsets even
                            colorless
with who taught you what and what not

        to eat and do and say
                doing it both ways
                with disregard to the
        professionally developed look

with the year of drying stolen
                neighbors' flowers
        female vocalists only
            beet soup
                        I was trying

with squinted past so it could radiate
                concentric out
                    to stay intact

with dry form
        chrysanthemums
        I grew up drinking
                tea of hardy petals that last
                well into the fall
        leave one feeling
                lengthened and alert

with nothing can stand alone
        the stranger yells me from the shore's edge
                where I collect
                stones yellow green blue and red
                    that all grey
                    out from water

to look at the whale bone
        just one vertebrae though
            too heavy to overturn
we place our palms on the surface
         let it sit heavy
to imagine an animal maneuvering
           largely and limbless

brother goes far out and always hated
        men like white fathers who
          could afford to say
            far out man

he's not dead but he's dead to me
            softly
            he's gold
        the way the women
        are perennials
        who come back every year

with the structure can be unbearable
    wanting one that's illusion
        not as in untrue but
        beauty a pattern
          not amounting

DIAMOND SCRAPS OF SOUTHEAST ALASKA, NORTHERN CALIFORNIA, NORTHWEST NEW MEXICO

Down the Frozen Yukon.   *Are No Longer Cannibals*
   The Alaska islands gen-   *erally are notable for their*
wealth and variety of flowers

      ,   *and almost all of these are fragrant.*
I can't be apart from the times   I can't be a part of the times

    times are mined extraction   times are wings pinned
The Aleutian Islands abound   *with them, and when the wind*
      is right the per ume

       can be noticed two or three
       miles off at sea.

   time placed her in the meadow   I mean the space between
    sidewalk and street   we butcher the name

In California taught to pick a poppy   is illegal taught to fear
its gold in synonyms and borders   *In Alaska*

    the polite name for the half   -   great-grandmother I am closest to you in
bust towns outnumbered by industry   men where women disappear
    are known to   sleeping with a knife under bed
though near the same relative height they joke I need a step ladder to get in the truck

    Growing regardless of California   Oregon Washington Nevada
    Arizona New Mexico Mexico

a considerable floating population,   *as in most Alaska villages, for the natives*
much resemble the Indians of the   *United States in their nomadic lives.*
The island of Kodiak is thickly wooded, and very attractive in appearance.

PLASTICITY MEDITATION

wear my hundred-dollar shoes   England leather-bound
made in Vietnam stretch tearing   up over one-hundred arrested
five states away   bind of a pipeline
forget bound as the past of bind   bind as in stuck ink on paper
bound as a born noun   acting outward future
my cow hide feet bind three states   his Purple Heart anger out
said my feet were native-shaped   good for running away

breathing I understand how this arises   breathing the fading of a problem

hungry I would eat one cheeseburger   a day in my car   oil and gas workers bound to
follow me after the complimentary   red lion breakfast would talk loud my
shape or shapelessness bind then follow   me to work today the buffalo came
out from the prairie into prairie I in desert   one buffalo I recall lone one
sullen in fog of Golden Gate Park bind or bound? how much water does
my body habit require?   please make my body
bound *for*
not to

SIR:

in this particular case it will be noted boss throws his arm
index pointed to mean look anywhere but at me he calls the
land his to cover land he calls   gnarly calls her   *old denim*
man and I both had slinged limbs weeks apart   then weeks
apart   panic

chalk green

trucks fenced

yard boat

helicoptered livestock

eagle on a doe carcass

how to approach underground roots spread fire   widowers
a trunk almost ash once in Albuquerque I threw out expired
boxes   swore quietly into a dumpster along the food bank
kids who   only ate   nonperishables during school day
hunger's

a wild horse

a nest of sage

weighted in stomach

that the alleged mother was an Indian

is it going to rain when he shouts I feel it in my bones when
one stopped dancing everyone became a ghost town I never
knew the name   if you brush an anthill with a finger onsite
you can find turquoise some ants attracted like some birds
attracted to blue   she dropped an instance into   a crease
my palm a day after I was fingerprinted   for a federal job
the cop and I   talked kindergarten   crafts   crime
snowflakes ethnicity   not fitting inside   the form gave me a
new draft   then showed me   a sink

Sincerely,

ATROCIOUS HORIZON

what made yellow   what made antlers shed   flower flower out

   a cactus in February   a doe   she'd handle
season   without handles is   out of bed before   plans to have

had sun   a lifetime left in pastime   is a cowboy man
   tugs his buckle out   a Chinese buffet at dusk   tangled hue

call the dig sites ours on file   letters with no tribal replies   drill sites
   asleep to gas station lights   sunflowers in the jar
coworkers get along fine well enough called yellow though habit kept

a live thing dead really   they're brown in the jar   the way out is
   far gone a buck in sun releases   testosterone I'm bleeding
in snow   a coworker boss' nephew wants me
   apologizes his jacket smells   like his trophy deer

leftover tracks a slow   pregnant with fear   I know where you live
saw over the weekend a red motel renovated after the oil boom

a former boss visits   talks about his jumpstarted   heart ketchup
mustard   annual javelina hunt   cases of beer   StairMaster

when I speak the federal   room laughs over my mother's labor
   how I came late   my supervisor   Head of Minerals
always says we're shooting   ourselves in the foot   here I wear
   my heart the sole of my   foot in mouth

hang dry   bouquet of wild thoughts thinking   this could've been
anything had I not   made it this this   could've been anything
had I not

NOT A CLOUD IN SIGHT

your dream color

labor and obstruction   silicon gave us search engines

neither here nor there   iron transcontinental railroad near Sacramento
                                         our birthday together on the train canned chili
                                         and tortilla chips cutting through the Sierra
                                         Mountain Range at the tops of trees the
                                         conductor makes a joke about gummy bears
                                         over the speaker then directs our eyes to a nest
                                         an eagle mother feeding recently hatched
                                         babies

pigs vs. peccary   when I get a tour of the Jicarilla National Forest
                                         coworkers tell me names for oil and gas well
                                         anatomies that's the pig the fire management
                                         officer called me into his cubicle and pretended
                                         to throw his prized javelina skull at me my
                                         hands cupped at my chest was pleased to phase
                                         me then insisted I hold it though the holding
                                         made him nervous I could feel the jaw was
                                         detachable I want to open it I give him some
                                         compliment

HOW YELLOW MEN STEAL OUR YELLOW STUFF

business-casual Levi's
safer than a dress
those who shoulder me
working
me with hands behind
an email body
DON'T BELIEVE
EVERYTHING
YOU HEAR
ABOUT ME!
      signed the Wildlife Tech

he states he gave
parakeets to a couple
of faggots on Craigslist
the lunch room laughs
missing cats and dogs
he blames on the
one Chinese restaurant
something like luck
in the name
his daughter named
Ginger

gold named for
yellow dawn
neutron stars
sank in molten earth
so malleable it
can be smashed
transparent

you *haven't shot a gun before?* pictures of galaxies and not having to be there minerals tech insisted on picking me up in his Ram mug with tricolor geometric wolves show me around cross Colorado we ran over a sparrow I read as the word *sorrow* rainbows of any amplitude rainbow in the sink the sparrow trapped his exhaust unopened letter from a dear friend he entered a dirt road toward a bluff all beige dried blue greenery sage and juniper blue all above that sometimes hurt to look verdigris steeples statues sweat under a heavy coat thrift collar button ups winter sun darkened my face red reeds against teal river I held his pistol heavier than expected shot at a bottle like a protagonist though I was more extra or dwindling river glass dump yard antique oil swirl a year signed away on government sheets expected to see the bullet trajectory as a result of my trigger

he took a   piss in plain sight   declarative shirts   you go
girl   earlier I stumbled down to a parched river bed   wildcat
canyon road   flamboyant socks   enough space enclosed   rot
scent of   deer before   I saw   her ribs   squatted on my good
leg   other extended   visible weather to talk about place   distance
a cloud streaks down a mountaintop   Fire   Management   Officer
told him to look out for me   sure to be a   heartbreaker   loose
tea a variety of petals could probably   drink any man   under the
table

said I   was not interested cartoon fruit depictions *don't worry you're   not that special*   six fray ends   stringed   instrument a lover   coiled once   he dropped me off   red L-shaped apartment complex   two-storied must've been a motel before when   oil flowed   essential oil aisle and not buying anything I lived   ground floor   pinned in the hinge of angle   upstairs neighbor every   finger   broken   hardly looked   like hands listened to *hey must   be the money* over and   over   knocked my door   he knew I lived alone tried to enter when he was loaded   I cooked   dinner in   a 45-pound   vest to pass the fire test   one hundred pushups a day and no   safer   hot and sour soup wood ear lily flower black   fungus   my mother   sent afraid of landlock how I   posed to correct   my limp   wanted to possess   soft of a horse mouth   and all that power

SW 6391 Gallant Gold	SW 2920 Monarch Gold	SW 9024 Vintage Gold	SW 6129 Restrained Gold	SW 6130 Mannered Gold	SW 6407 Ancestral Gold
View Details	View Details	View Details	View Details	View Details	View Details
SW 6401 Independent Gold	SW 2814 Rockwood Antique Gold	SW 7700 Olde World Gold	SW 6677 Goldenrod	SW 6905 Goldfinch	SW 6664 Marigold
View Details	View Details	View Details	View Details	View Details	View Details

MECHANICAL BULL

From a hotel window the refinery lights are a false reflection of the night sky they obscure below what I know are mountains in day. I resist my impulse to find the lights pretty.

Opaque curtains over the sheer ones and then decidedly glass and wakefulness.

A plaque interrupts the wedding ceremony's panorama of El Paso—Juárez. A cement block to claim the Franklin Mountains as the southernmost part of the Rockies, as if that's what makes them credible as mountains. As if land starts over at the border. As if land decides to be in allegiance.

As if language didn't happen like a leak. A slow extension of ow and mm.

Earlier the server asked the group where in Asia we're from. Reminded us how close we are to Mexico. The *ll* denotes an absence of itself and the *rr* duplicates in the mouth.

The dove sound the guitarist made exits his throat and lands in my sternum. Song about the man who left his wife for someone younger, only to return years later to his wife.

--

My father, blacked out, mimicked my mother's dead mother, switching l's and r's. Didn't stop as her tears disappeared against the varnish of our mahogany table.

This memory crystallizes, while others I learned to forget. The times he chased and threw me against walls. Commented on the shape of my teenage legs as I put dishes away. The hollow echo of a lock I had on my bedroom door.

--

A phoneme is missing or it never had to exist.

My grandmother was a mail-order bride from Hong Kong, decades younger than my grandfather. She worked at a candy factory in Oakland. When enough of her fingers were taken by machines, she opened a daycare in the family house. My mother, eyes glassy, told me she saw my grandfather molesting a young girl. That he impregnated his underage niece. After she gave birth, the family had her tubes tied as punishment.

And the niece's brother, the myth of him singing in San Quentin. *Why was he there? Something he did to his wife.*

The fathers, under a patina of nostalgia—their wrongdoings covered by all they endured as orphans in the hands of men. My grandfather's beautiful Cantonese on the cardboard that holds the Christmas manger. His lute. Birthday winter-melon soup in August. Loose tobacco on scrapes. Meditation chimes. The jug of red wine. He would get the garbage man drunk the morning of pick-up. The tomato he packed for lunch to be eaten as an apple. A small, un-American offense.

--

Copper extracted from the earth, with the potential to conduct electricity, graces steeples. The verdigris oxidation stuns. Looking greener against blue sky and bluer against grey. Copper turns into its complementary color.

--

The wedding guests are promised a mechanical bull, though it doesn't appear. Slot of coins for the bull that, if there, wouldn't have legs. Laundry quarters for loose change we don't carry anymore. Buffalo nickel my mother gave me that I lost. Checked all my little wooden and tortoise shell boxes. A sentimental rubberneck container of letters, postcards, ticket stubs, rocks I carry to each state. It wasn't there.

--

The nickel was first called an Indian Head. Called nickel though it is 75% copper.

There were disputes about how the ridges of the design would fit into coin-operated machines.

--

A cashier at El Cometa speaks to my twin and me quickly in Spanish, to which I say sorry for my ambiguity. That I refer to you as cashier. You as machinery.

--

Lonely to know you can't disappoint me in your absence: father, grandfather, grandmother, great-grandmother, great-grandfather, and on and on.

I can't help noticing paint jobs on buildings. Generations of pastel choices over adobe the weather reclaims as earth color.

--

My father was a housepainter in San Francisco during the 70s after hitchhiking his way from New York. When they painted Anchor Brewing Company they drank from the discarded bottles the machines didn't fill completely. Drunk on the scaffolds. Free love. The promise of exotic land, women, and children. Liquid gold. Eventually, he had his own small company. I bragged about our German last name on white trucks. He bragged about what he got away with.

We lived on Castro Street in the 90s, gentrifying the queer neighborhood. A magenta burn on my knee formed like a continent when I was four. My father put ammonia on my scrape. I never minded the mistake, but in my family we had to call it a birthmark to protect my father's feelings. My father threw me outside when I cried at night. The slide sound of the bolt when I got to the front door. The burn turns red in warm weather and purple in the cold.

--

Following through with a scorched earth policy, the United States government left the buffalo they killed to rot. The skulls were gathered into unthinkably large piles. They were processed into glue and dye. They were processed into bone char. Ash that decolorized (or "refined") sugar into purity.

At my father's warehouse, the sugar cubes lined inside neat cardboard boxes next to the coffee. We put the cubes in our mouths and waited for them to turn from gravel to silt. All the factories and businesses were across the Caltrain tracks. We walked through the opening in the bushes and crossed the tracks to get home.

The smell of processing chocolate at dusk added a richness to our neighborhood games. Barefoot in the streets, riding bikes, climbing the maple tree.

I resist my impulse to like the smell of oil, of paint fumes, of varnish.

--

Leland Stanford, who served as Governor of California, Senator of the United States, and President of the Central Pacific Railroad, depended on the Chinese laborers he debased: *Asia with her numberless millions sends to her shores the dregs of her population. There can be no doubt that the presence of numbers of the degraded and distinct people will exercise a deleterious influence upon the superior race.*

At the center of the hotel banquet hall, the party finds relief in automated line dances: Copperhead Road, The Electric Slide, The Wobble. Assembly lines of joy.

--

The blow of the horn bisects towns into industrial and suburban.

How the news story covered the Indiana train crash that *pronounced* my childhood next-door neighbor *dead*. Her mother can't go to weddings. *The impact sent personal items flying*—as if this softens the image of what happened to her 22-year-old self.

At first, I thought of her hands when we were children, interlaced in mine. The white marks above the cuticles she said had to do with an excess, or absence, of vitamins. I didn't own a black dress, so my mother lent me her mother's. This is the closest I ever felt to my grandmother, mourning a friend. At the reception table, the fathers wanted me to stand and, in the heaviness of my grief, give them all a spin.

The lowering device placed her and her casket into a gravesite in Colma, a town where there are more dead than living—where my great-grandmother is buried.

This primes my move to New Mexico where I eventually land my first salaried job in forestry. Days before moving, I fell asleep to the feeling of panic and the image of my nails digging into muddy snow. The knowledge of two men behind me with guns. I ignored this lucid dream, rushing to escape my alcoholic household where I was recovering from surgery. The burn on my knee gained three scars.

--

Babies already know how to dance. A tug of war of dependence onto the slippery floor. It's the adults who string themselves self-conscious to one another.

The night carries on with a back and forth of *I saw you earlier but didn't say hello*.

I'm comforted in this dull ritual. That some of what is lost will return.

RESTRAINED GOLD 6129

How many chickens did your family own?
Personal leave days

How many fingers did your mother have?
Removal proceedings

What is your milk name?
Vacancy

What was your high school mascot?
To advance the mission

What is your father's middle name?
Uniform allowance

Did you ever hear him called by any other name?
Employee recognition program

What was the first concert you attended?
Movement of people and goods into

What is the name of the first person you kissed?
A personal contribution

What was the name of the sister that died?
General public

Didn't you ever hear that you had had a brother?
Ten paid holidays per year

What was the color of your dreams?
Criminal aliens

Then how do you know you lived with him?

NO NAME

nations are competing to re-walk on the moon
bottle the unseen water   I can see the moon
this morning tucked halfway in the doubtless
blue sky   blue is the thing in itself
while the moon carbon copied is the naming of it

                              I don't always see a point
wording around words
                              my brother considered
erasing our father from his name weeks ago
but didn't see how that would alter
the present by way of the past

in the news there's a quantity to the grief
numbers of deaths   acres of land

                              California named after
          some myth about dark Queen Calafia
ruling dark ladies on an island east of Asia

every time a hawk flies over I say *wow*
and point like its mine

what is the word for this blue so blue
you can consider the idea of purple

NOTES

This is an incomplete list of language, imagery, and information the poems were written and conceptualized alongside. The quotes do not necessarily indicate the precise site of inspiration, but serve, after-the-fact, as points of reference and suggested further readings and viewings. Some of the texts I encountered after the poems were written.

◊

Bergognone, Ambrogio. *The Assumption of the Virgin*. 1453-1523. Oil and gold on wood. Metropolitan Museum of Art, New York.

The poem that begins "-- oOo -- two bored and diligent angels crown a virgin / rolling her eyes" is a reference to this painting and the following.

Buddha, Probably Amitabha (Amituofo). Tang Dynasty (618-907). Hollow dry lacquer with traces of gilt and polychrome pigment and gilding. Metropolitan Museum of Art, New York.

◊

Cajete, Gregory. *Native Science: Natural Laws of Interdependence*. Santa Fe: Clear Light Publishers, 2016.

The poem "the scent of a herbs is a plant screaming in flames" was written alongside this text and Cajete's perspective and knowledge on entropy.

◊

California Dept. of Parks and Recreation. California Exotic Pest Plant Council. "Focused Environmental Study: Restoration of Angel Island Natural Areas Affected by Eucalyptus." *Cal-IPC*. California State Parks, 1997.

The poem "stunning angel island fire seen for miles" takes from this Cal-IPC study. Its title is from an article by Tanya Schevitz in the *SFGate*.

◊

Deloria, Philip J. *Playing Indian*. New Haven: Yale University Press, 1998.

"As Indian words and expressions spread into proto-American discourse, they subtly shifted the ways in which colonists understood themselves and their world. The most important of these linguistic intruders was metaphor, a language trick that suggests the continual shifting, replacement, and doubling of ideas and identities. Colonists thought that native languages lacked the descriptive power of English and had to rely on the almost continual use of metaphor to describe abstract ideas. Accordingly, they adopted it as a general way of signifying Indianness" (33).

◊

Deloria Jr., Vine. *The World We Used to Live In: Remembering the Powers of the Medicine Men*. Golden, CO: Fulcrum Publishing, 2006.

My disorientation with months, time, and place throughout the book were given some grounding from the last book Deloria wrote in regard to Indigenous concepts of time and place as well as dreams.

"Birds and animals were true to their breed, and while different birds made different nests, birds as a group were restricted to using a certain general pattern in creating a dwelling place and raising their offspring. This belief in the orderliness of things, regardless of the apparent chaos, represents the spiritual side of life—how spirit manifests itself in the physical world" (xxix).

◊

Dobie, Charles Caldwell. *San Francisco's Chinatown*. New York: D. Appleton-Century Company, 1936.

Hong Ah Wing, my great-grandfather, (or another Hong who was a chef and gang member murdered around the same time), appears in the introduction as a troubling metaphor for Chinese immigrants and their relationship to poverty, space, and beauty. I found this at the University of Arizona library, and it sat on my desk for months. I had a fever and decided to open the book to serendipitously find my great-grandfather (or his double). I thought I was hallucinating. The Methodist mission home (now called Gum Moon Residence Hall) also appears in this book. My Alaska Native great-grandmother died there where primarily Chinese women and girls resided as refuge to the male-dominated, post-Gold Rush San Francisco. Hong Ah Wing's murder appeared in the *San Francisco Call* (1890-1913), which I accessed from the California Digital Newspaper Collection.

◊

Foster, Josephine. *Graphic As A Star*. London: Fire Records, 2009.

Many early drafts were written with this album in which Foster sings Emily Dickinson poems. The star quilt appears on the cover. I originally tried to organize this book into the pattern of a star quilt, but the poems resisted form and order.

Long Soldier, Layli. *Whereas*. Minneapolis: Graywolf Press, 2017.

Long Soldier's investigative poetics influenced my approach to federal documents, which is particularly evident in the poem "to ward." At a recent reading, I learned that Long Soldier has been working on a more cohesive (literally and figuratively), culturally-centered star quilt project than the abandoned, culturally-scattered attempt I made. You can view "Quilts" online by the Poetry Foundation for a glimpse into this stunning work.

◊

Gonzales, Patrisia. *Red Medicine: Traditional Indigenous Rites of Birthing and Healing*. Tucson: University of Arizona Press, 2012.

Many of the poems I wrote while taking graduate courses taught by Dr. Patrisia Gonzales on traditional healing and medicine making. Many of my reference to herbs and plants come from these teachings.

◊

Hartman, Saidiya. *Lose Your Mother: A Journey Along the Atlantic Slave Route*. New York: Farrar, Straus and Giroux, 2007.

On finding her maternal great-great-grandmother's "slave testimony" in Alabama archives, Hartman writes: "Were gaps and silences and empty rooms the substance of my history? If ruin was my sole inheritance and the only certainty the impossibility of recovering the stories of the enslaved, did this make my history tantamount to mourning? Or worse, was it a melancholia I would never be able to overcome? 'I do not know my father.' 'I have lost my mother.' 'My children are scattered in every direction.' These were common refrains in the testimony" (15).

◊

Hastings, Lansford W. *The Emigrants' Guide to Oregon and California*. Cincinnati: G. Conclin, 1845.

I quote this white settler instruction manual in italics proceeding the titles "resolve," "I will furnish a man," "US flag inverted," "welcome sign facing in," "kindly disposition when broken," and "moved for California weather." The poems came out of a decombining writing exercise coined by poet Farid Matuk. I intentionally induced afterimages to inform my poetics with CAConrad's (soma)tic poetry rituals in mind. In the attempt to regain control of my sight, while reading about violence inflicted on immigrants and Indigenous people, past and present, I stared at a chosen color and then at a blank page or one of my poems to see the afterimage flash in the white space. The act would coax me into re-entering poems, texts, and archival material.

◊

Hinton, Leanne. *Flutes of Fire: Essays on California Indian Languages*. Berkeley: Heyday Books, 1994.

The poem "Lessen" came to exist with this text.

"[California Indian communities'] survival is especially amazing when we realize that it is now over two centuries since the deeply disruptive establishment of the Spanish missions, and nearly a century and a half since the Gold Rush and its tragic aftermath. But despite their endurance, the California languages are at the brink of extinction. The fifty living languages are what remain of around a hundred spoken here in 1800" (21).

"[T]he Wintu language conveys a sense of humans as individuals, in that they are not to be coerced or owned, while English often asserts relationship as ownership" (64).

◊

Infante Lyons, Linda. *St. Katherine of Karluk*. 2016. Oil on panel. Alutiiq Museum, Kodiak.

I reference this portrait of the artist's great-grandmother as well as the TV series *Life Below Zero* in "two colors diametrically opposed."

◊

Kimmerer, Robin Wall. *Braiding Sweetgrass: Indigenous Wisdom, Scientific Knowledge, and the Teachings of Plants*. Minneapolis: Milkweed Editions, 2013.

I wrote many poems alongside these essays. The chapter "Asters and Goldenrod" helped reinforce my afterimage writing ritual.

"Color perception in humans relies on banks of specialized receptor cells, the rods and cones in the retina. The job of the cone cells is to absorb light of different wavelengths and pass it on to the brain's visual cortex, where it can be interpreted. The visible light spectrum, the rainbow of colors, is broad, so the most effective means of discerning color is not one generalized jack-of-all-trades cone cell, but rather an array of specialists, each perfectly tuned to absorb certain wavelengths. The human eye has three kinds. One type excels at detecting red and associated wavelengths. One is turned blue. The other optimally perceives light of two colors: purple and yellow" (45).

◊

Lindsay, Brendan C. *Murder State: California's Native American Genocide, 1846-1873*. Lincoln: University of Nebraska Press, 2012.

Gratitude to my California childhood friend Devin Briski who, upon hearing about my project, immediately ordered this book for me.

"Perhaps worst of all, local governments acted as something akin to governing boards of avaricious homeowners associations in response to their constituencies' demands, as local leaders and authorities petitioned the state for arms and money to kill Indians, set scalp and head bounties, and looked the other way as their citizens kidnapped, raped, and murdered local Native people. Taken together the acts of local, regional, and state governments in California show them to be complicit in the genocide of Native American peoples" (28).

"This cycle of starvation of Native peoples, their stock theft for food, and the bloody, retaliatory vengeance by settlers and ranchers, exacted often with self-righteous fury, was the key sequence of events leading to the Euro-American claim that extermination of Indigenous populations was a practical necessity" (183).

◊

L'Oréal Paris. *Colour Riche*. 2017.

Some of the language throughout comes from nail polish and makeup names and online reviews.

◊

Sherwin-Williams. *Find & Explore Colors*.

I spent much of my childhood looking at and reading paint fan decks because my father had a house painting company. Many of this book's poem titles and language come from this deck. The poet Clare McLane kindly lent me her paint fan deck.

◊

Staley, Jeffrey L. " 'Gum Moon': The First Fifty Years of Methodist Women's Work in San Francisco Chinatown, 1870-1920." *The Argonaut*. Volume 16:1 (2005) pp. 4-25. June 2019.

The last photo of the book comes from this article that covers the Gum Moon Women's Residence, which was the Methodist Mission home in San Francisco Chinatown where my great-grandmother lived and died. I found this by researching Marguerite Lake (standing second to left in the photo) who was a missionary for the "Oriental Bureau" during the time my great-grandmother was there and had her children. The woman standing on the far left could be my great-grandmother based on image and date alone.

◊

United States. U.S. Dept. of Agriculture. *Where the Moon Trees Grow*. NASA. 14 Jan. 2014.

Ed Cliff, chief of the Forest Service in the 1970s, had the idea for Apollo 14 astronauts to take more than 500 tree seeds with them when they circled the moon as an experiment, but mostly a publicity stunt, to see if the seeds would grow on Earth after "being exposed to the harsh realities of space travel, including zero gravity and radiation." Of the original 500, 450 seeds sprouted and were transplanted to government-designated spaces. I view this as a gross colonial, Euro-westerner display of decadence and energy. These trees have plaques, while many Indigenous people and communities have been literally burned and covered on the very same land with no recognition of this violence.

◊

United States. U.S. Dept. of Commerce and Labor. Immigration Service. *Hong On*. United States
     Immigration Service Chinese Division Angel Island, CA. 1912. Reproduced at the National
     Archives-Pacific Region. 2012.

Much of the language and driving force behind this book stems from the immigration trial of my grandfather. My brother, Gus Meuschke, an academic and artist, led us to the archive in 2012, and it has been haunting us ever since.

◊

United States. U.S. Immigration and Customs Enforcement. *Frequently Asked Questions (FAQs)*. 2017.

Some of the language in the poem "restrained gold 6129" comes from this site.

◊

Yellowbird, Michael. "Neurodecolonization: using mindfulness practices to delete the neural
     networks of colonialism." *For Indigenous Minds Only: A Decolonization Handbook*. Santa Fe:
     School of American Research, 2012.

The poem "plasticity meditation" came from a meditation exercise in Yellowbird's handbook.

"In 'Relieving Our Suffering: Indigenous Decolonization and a United States Truth Commission,' Waziyatawin argues that as Indigenous Peoples we can empower ourselves and initiate our own healing processes from historical or contemporary injustices by speaking the truth about those injustices" (6).

ACKNOWLEDGMENTS

Thank you to the following journals and editors for publishing some of these poems: *BOAAT Journal*, *The Brooklyn Rail*, *Contra Viento*, *Fence Magazine*, *The Sonora Review*, and *Zócalo Magazine*. Thank you to the *Western Humanities Review* and Oliver de la Paz for selecting "an iridescent stone I don't recall the name of" as the Mountain West Contest winner in the winter 2015 issue. Thank you to *LandLocked Magazine* (formerly *Beecher's Magazine*) and CAConrad for selecting "atrocious horizon" as the contest winner in spring 2016.

Thank you to the University of Arizona Creative Writing MFA for providing time, space, and writerly kinship as well as an escape from the U.S. Forest Service. Acceptance to the program emboldened me to leave and offered hope during a bleak time.

This book wouldn't exist without the influence of Susan Briante and Farid Matuk.

Thank you to my workshop cohort. I wrote many of these poems trying to mimic and impress you: Taneum Bambrick, Jos Charles, Charlie D'eve, Gabriel Dozal, Deb Gravina, Raquel Gutiérrez, Clare McClane, Kou Sugita, Liam Swanson, Gabriel Palacios, and Peyton Prater-Stark.

I'm grateful to the writers and teachers who heavily influenced my poetics early on: Anselm Berrigan, Christian Hawkey, Ellen Levy, Anna Moschovakis, and Tracy Grinnell. Thank you for showing me ways to live as a poet.

Thank you to Las Milpitas Community Farm for offering a lush space during my editing process. I learned approaches to knowledge-sharing and editing techniques by way of garden tasks along the Santa Cruz River.

Thank you to the intelligent and thorough editor Diana Arterian, and all at Noemi Press who made this book happen.

Thank you to Linda Infante Lyons whose art is featured on this book's cover. Visit lindainfantelyons.com to see more of her work.

Thank you to Will Stanier, founder of i.e. Press, who made a chapbook, also entitled *Upend*, with several of these poems.

Thank you to the poet Paul Bisagni for comradery and inspiration throughout the span of this book—for a stream of film, poetry, and female vocalist recommendations—for dream re-tellings and long walks—for avian stories—all of which make a world I want to write through.

Thank you to my family for nurturing me and for surviving our legacy—for choosing gentleness over violence—my mother, Judy Meuschke—my uncles and aunts, Ed Hong, Ai Hong, Betty Hong, and Raymond Hong—my siblings, Nicole Meuschke and Gus Meuschke—my cousin, Cooper Hong.